Inspired by Trees

Creative Workbook

Wellbeing for you and our world

Sarah Spencer
Eva Spencer

"To such an extent does nature delight and abound in variety that among her trees there is not one plant to be found which is exactly like another; and not only among the plants, but among the boughs, the leaves and the fruits, you will not find one which is exactly similar to another."
~ Leonardo da Vinci

This book belongs to

_ _ _ _ _ _ _ _ _ _ _ _

Hello!

Welcome to this creative workbook. We're Sarah and Eva, mother and daughter, from Derbyshire in the National Forest, UK. We love spending time outdoors learning from, and being inspired by, trees and other living beings.

We hope that the activities in this book will help you to:

☐ *Connect with trees*

Spending time in nature has numerous benefits for health and wellbeing. Studies show that connecting with nature has benefits for your heart, breathing, immune system and can decrease symptoms of many illnesses. It's good for sleep too. Nature-connection improves mental wellbeing - through increased happiness, but it also improves the wellbeing that comes with self-acceptance, personal growth and finding meaning and purpose in life. However, to feel the maximum benefit you need to pause, observe, listen and learn from what the living world is telling you. Think about this in terms of moments spent creating relationships with other living beings, not simply minutes spend in the outdoors.

☐ *Make changes to lead a more conscious life*

Conscious living involves looking at ourselves and our lifestyle with new eyes, considering the likely outcomes of our actions and making appropriate changes.
Some simple changes are suggested throughout the book.

Conscious living encompasses these aspects:
- care for the earth (eco and nature-friendly living - at home, at work, during leisure, and within communities, with regard to our impact on the world)
- care for ourself (self-compassion, personal development and the formation of firm foundations for playing a positive role in the world)
- care for other people (our family, friends, neighbours, colleagues and people we don't know personally)
- care for future generations (our own descendants, those of other people, and future generations of all living beings).

☐ *Learn from nature's wisdom via a set of natural principles*

All living beings share patterns that have evolved over billions of years. These are the secrets of success for:

- finding purpose
- growth and success
- building resilience
- creating ideal conditions to thrive
- developing positive relationships
- leaving a lasting legacy

Because we are part of the living world, we can learn from these natural principles. The best way to benefit from them is to:

- head outdoors to observe each one in nature
- think what you can learn from that principle for your own life.

There are natural principles throughout the book. They look like this:

Value your uniqueness

Every living being on our diverse planet is unique. In the living world, diversity means health, growth, creativity, vitality and resilience, so you should see your own uniqueness as being of the highest value. You can apply the same principle to others by valuing diversity.

☐ *Have courage to change your world and the world around you*

Nature teaches us that even the smallest organisms change the world. Think of the first bacteria that lived 3.8 billion years ago. It was the start of all the wonderful diversity of life on our planet. Be inspired by trees. They are changing the soil, the climate, the air and the water around them. They are part of forests that create rain and unique microclimates. Sometimes we feel we are too small to make a difference, but trees give us the confidence to be the change we want to see in the world...

"Trees are sanctuaries.
Whoever knows how to speak to them,
whoever knows how to listen to them,
can learn the truth.
They do not preach learning and precepts,
they preach, undeterred by particulars,
the ancient law of life."
~ Hermann Hesse

Be creative!

Creativity is making something new, personal, unique and meaningful.
Everyone has their own unique creativity and this workbook is for you alone, so don't hold back! There is no right or wrong way to use it.

The exercises are tried and tested and proven to improve wellbeing for you and for our world, but they don't work if you don't do them, so remember to take this book, pens and coloured pencils with you whenever you head outdoors.

You can use this workbook to:

Look	Create	Appreciate	Plan
Listen	Craft	Write	List
Think	Experience	Transform	Collect
Love	Pause	Doodle	Journal
Smell	Be inspired	Wonder	Explore
Draw	Touch	Colour	Reflect
Discover	Ponder	Relax	Take action
Feel	Grow		
Connect	Change		

"A painter told me that nobody could draw a tree without in some sort becoming a tree..."
– Ralph Waldo Emerson

Find your nearby nature spaces

List ten places near to you…
They don't need to be big – just a few trees or plants can inspire you.

1.

2.

3.

4.

5.

6

7.

8.

9.

10.

Conscious living:

Think about your impact on the places you visit.
This includes your travel choices, what you disturb, what you take away and what you leave behind.
Here are some ideas:

- ☐ Walk, cycle or use public transport
- ☐ Take your own water bottle and packed lunch (this avoids single-use plastic)
- ☐ Take everything home with you
- ☐ If you pick or forage consider the impact of doing so
- ☐ Think about where you're walking - keep out of protected areas or spaces with rare or unusual plants or wildlife
- ☐ Leave gates as you find them or as signposted
- ☐ Follow countryside rules

"The weeds in a city convey the same lessons as the redwoods."
- Aldo Leopold

Observe and interact

Trees are constantly perceiving the world around them. They use their amazing senses to inform their actions. We humans often go about our daily lives without paying full attention to the world around us. Perhaps we are thinking about our daily routine, or distracted by our worries. Usually we favour some of our senses (such as sight) more than others and have to make a conscious effort to use those that are less familiar (for example listening for a full range of sounds, or touching a variety of different textured natural objects.) The 'observe and interact' natural principle encourages us to use our full range of senses, including tuning-into our emotions, so that we have more of the information necessary to make the best choices about how to live.

Explore the living world. Use all of your senses. What can you see, hear, smell, touch? Try switching between your senses and imagine that you are experiencing the sensation for the very first time.

How do you feel?
Try to immerse yourself in nature without judgement.

"A fool sees not the same tree
that a wise man sees."
~ William Blake

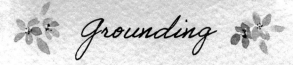

Grounding

Find a green space. You can take off your shoes if you wish, to experience the sensation of your bare feet on the ground.

Take a moment to stretch your body, noticing any areas of tightness and any areas that need to be released. Wiggle your fingers and toes, tense and release your muscles to let go of tension.

Take a deep breath in and, as you breathe out, bring yourself to an easy balanced stance, with your feet slightly apart. Take a few more deep breaths.

Close your eyes and feel your feet on the ground with gravity pulling you into the earth. Think about what it means to be rooted to this spot on a planet that is revolving in space.

Imagine you have roots extending from your feet into the earth. Breathe deeply and, as you breathe out, imagine pushing your roots through the soil, connecting with roots of trees and plants, and with other organisms. When you bring yourself back to your regular breathing pattern, spend some time rooted to the spot, feeling that connection below and above ground.

Take a deep breath in and, as you breathe out, release any worries or concerns that you don't want right now. Visualise them flowing away on the breeze.

Take another deep breath in and draw up strength, inspiration and passion from your roots under the ground. Feel your spine grow as this feeling moves through your body.

Raise your arms above your head and then extend them slightly to the side. These are your branches. Stand tall and face the day with the strength of a tree.

"I go to nature to be soothed and healed,
and to have my senses put in tune once more."
- John Burroughs

"There is no such thing as bad weather,
only unsuitable clothing"

Checklist

All year round:

- ☐ Boots or strong shoes
- ☐ Comfortable clothes
- ☐ Layers of tops (that you can take on and off as the weather changes)
- ☐ Waterproof backpack
- ☐ Water bottle
- ☐ Snacks or packed lunch
- ☐ This workbook
- ☐ Sketchbook, notebook or journal
- ☐ Pen, pencil, coloured pencils
- ☐ Phone – for emergencies but also for taking photos, recording sounds, taking videos (but try to turn it off when you don't need it)
- ☐ Small first aid kit
- ☐ Any medication you need
- ☐ Map, compass
- ☐ Emergency kit for longer hikes

Rain:

- ☐ Raincoat
- ☐ Waterproof boots
- ☐ Waterproof trousers
- ☐ Rain hat (better than a hood because you can look around more easily)
- ☐ Waterproof bag
- ☐ Change of socks

Shine:

- ☐ Sun hat
- ☐ Suncream (but don't slap it on unnecessarily – you need your Vitamin D)
- ☐ Bare feet?
- ☐ Thin, fold-away waterproof (in case of rain but also to sit on)

Cold:

- ☐ Woolly hat
- ☐ Scarf
- ☐ Gloves
- ☐ Warm, waterproof coat
- ☐ Thermal under-trousers
- ☐ Extra pair of socks
- ☐ Flask of hot drink or soup

Extras:

When you're out in nature, close your eyes and notice the smells around you. How do the smells change according to the weather?

Conscious living:

Avoid buying new clothing and equipment. Search the back of your wardrobe, check out charity or thrift shops and ask your friends. If you buy new, invest in clothing that is made from natural materials and of good quality, that will last.

Take a reusable water bottle and a flask or reusable mug for hot drinks. Take a packed lunch or stop at a local cafe rather than buying take-away items in disposable packaging.

"An early morning walk is a blessing for the whole day."
- Henry David Thoreau

3 good things in nature everyday

Each day notice three good things in nature. Write a simple sentence and sketch or photograph each good thing.

Saturday

Sunday

Monday

Tuesday

Wednesday

Thursday

Friday

Noting three good things in nature has been proven to
improve wellbeing by researchers at Derby University UK

When I was a child...

Recall a childhood encounter with the living world. Describe the sights, sounds, smells, feelings and emotions.

How have your early experiences of being outdoors influenced your life?

You might like to turn these thoughts into a song, nursery rhyme, story or fable. You could even share your story or song with a child so they can benefit from your love of nature.

Leave wild spaces in your life

There are many pressures in the modern world to fill every waking hour with activities - planning our lives and filling our schedules. Making time to daydream, to 'do nothing' and to be bored leaves spaces for reflection, relaxation and seeing life from new perspectives. These times can be opportunities for inspiration and creativity. Seeing the value in the 'wild' can help us leave behind anxiety-inducing ideas of tidiness and 'perfection'. You can also create wild spaces in your garden and local area.

"What would the world be, once bereft
Of wet and of wilderness? Let them be left,
O let them be left, wildness and wet;
Long live the weeds and the wilderness yet."
- Gerard Manley Hopkins

Continue to grow

Trees continue to grow through changing circumstances. We can use this natural principle as a motivation not to give up when times are tough. It is also an invitation to continue to learn and improve ourselves throughout our lives. This could include education and learning, gaining new skills, keeping our minds and bodies active and investing in tools for wellbeing.

Think of some ideas for your growth and personal development.
Add each one as a flower on the stems below.

"One can choose to go back toward safety
or forward toward growth.
Growth must be chosen again and again;
fear must be overcome again and again."
- Abraham Maslow

Find slow and small solutions

We are often encouraged to choose 'quick-fix' solutions to issues, such as losing weight, getting fit or finding happiness. We can be inspired by trees which take a long-term approach. Knowing that slow and small solutions are more successful can help us maintain momentum when results are slow to materialise.

Conscious living:

There are many changes you can make to slow down, relocalise and simplify your life. Here are some ideas, and space to add your own:

- ☐ Declutter (but don't throw out useful items that can be used to make or repair, such as tools or craft items)
- ☐ Design a long-term healthy-eating plan
- ☐ Put money aside each month for items you need rather than relying on credit
- ☐ Check out 'Hygge', a Danish concept, meaning a feeling of cosiness or charm. Create special moments to appreciate the time you have right now with present company
- ☐ Shop locally - keep money circulating in your local commmunity
- ☐ Write a list of simple pleasures
- ☐ Devise a long-term fitness plan that is realistic and achievable. Build fitness step-by-step and include rewards at each stage
- ☐ Shift your thinking to appreciate what you have, rather than ruminating about what you don't have
- ☐ Avoid adverts, commercials and competitive peer-pressure that encourage you to want more, bigger and more expensive
- ☐ If you want to make life-changes, prepare a plan that considers different options, and take things one stage at a time rather than making huge changes all at once
- ☐ Check out the slow food movement - choose local sustainable restaurants and take time over meals, rather than eating fast-food
- ☐ Avoid fast-fashion - buy high-quality items that will last and that you will want to wear again and again. Rent clothes rather than buying new.
- ☐ Find joy and satisfaction in being creative
- ☐ Seek out friends and networks of people who share the same outlook

"Adopt the pace of nature, her secret is patience."
~Ralph Waldo Emerson

Waste nothing, recycle everything

Nothing is wasted in nature. Circular systems ensure that everything no longer needed by one organism is used by others. This natural principle encourages you to think about what you are wasting in your life - time, opportunities, friendships?   What can you do to waste less and to recycle your experiences into new ones?

Conscious living:

Here is a hierarchy of ways to waste less.
Add your own ideas to each category.
Commit to these changes today.

»   Refuse (refuse to buy things you don't need)
☐
☐

»   Reduce (reduce the amount you consume)
☐
☐

»   Reuse (reuse things you already have instead of buying new)
☐
☐

»   Repurpose (give old items a new life)
☐
☐

»   Recycle (turn waste products into something else)
☐
☐

»   Rot (turn food and garden waste into useful compost)
☐
☐

Catch and use energy effectively

All living things are ultimately powered by sunlight. Trees use the energy they capture during photosynthesis carefully, expending it only where needed, and storing it for the future. Investments in our own energy levels include nutritious food, rest, relaxation and appropriate exercise. Things that sap energy include lack of sleep, stress, environmental factors and mental and physical illnesses.

How could you manage your energy levels more effectively?

"Manage your energy, not your time."

Energy choices

Conscious living:

Our modern human world is powered mainly by ancient sunlight, via plants that lived hundreds of millions of years ago. These ancient energy stores are known as fossil fuels. However, for 3.8 billion years, non-human organisms have been fuelled by the sun shining at the time, or stored for very short periods. Renewables and energy-saving practices mimic nature's successes, allowing us to play our part in keeping our climate and biosphere in balance, which creates a home that is habitable to millions of species (including us!).

By making conscious choices we, as individuals, can play our part in creating balance in our climate, complementing the silent work of trees.

Which of these can you commit to? Add a timescale to each one you choose.

- ☐ Switch to a renewable electricity provider
- ☐ Insulate your loft
- ☐ Install an electricity meter or buy a monitor that shows your energy use in real time
- ☐ Turn off lights and other electrical items when you're not using them
- ☐ Look for zero electicity and zero waste alternatives to electrical items (eg toothbrushes, hair stylers, floor cleaners, leaf blowers and all those tools and gadgets we can do without)
- ☐ Choose efficient appliances
- ☐ Air-dry your laundry and skip ironing
- ☐ Research ground-source and air-source heat pumps, and other sources of renewable energy for your home
- ☐ Use human power for transport where possible - walk or cycle
- ☐ If you do have a car, cut down on its use
- ☐ Ditch unnecessary flying - holiday closer to home
- ☐ Make your next car electric
- ☐ Change any private investments or pension out of fossil fuels and into ethical investment products. Join or start a campaign for your company pensions to divest from fossil fuels
- ☐ Join a community-owned power scheme
- ☐ Encourage your bosses to conduct an energy-efficiency audit of your workplace
- ☐ Join a campaign for a fossil-free future
- ☐ Install solar panels (just like a tree!)
- ☐ Check out www.52climateactions.com for more ideas

Follow nature's patterns

Patterns are repeated throughout nature because they offer benefits and have demonstrated their success over millions of years. They allow growth, flexibility and adaptability, and offer strength, efficiency and resilience. We can learn from these patterns for our own lives.

Find examples of patterns in nature. Draw what you find, noticing the details and characteristics of each pattern.

- *Where can you see that pattern in your own life?*
- *What can you learn from that pattern?*

Example:

Branching patterns can be seen in:

- *leaves and twigs*
- *our own veins and capillaries*
- *networks of family and friends*
- *We can learn to invest in diverse friendships and family relationships so we have many different sources of mutual support in difficult times.*

Branching patterns...

Honeycomb or bubble patterns...

Use your edge

The most fertile spaces in nature are often found between two different ecosystems. For plants and animals in this zone there are huge benefits, but there are also risks associated with entering new ground. Stepping outside of your comfort zone opens up opportunities for creativity and new experiences. Remember that when breaking new ground, there will be setbacks (which we can try to view as opportunities), but trying will always be better than never having put yourself out there.

Comfort zone challenge

What can you do this week to put yourself outside of your comfort zone?
It's ok if it doesn't work out as planned – it's all about giving it a go...
Keep a photo or draw a sketch of you completing your challenge.

Be a good ancestor

Trees show us that our strongest purpose should be to try to be the best ancestor that we can. The Native American idea of seven-generation-thinking imposes a duty to consider the impact of every decision on the seventh generation into the future. Each day we can ask ourselves, will this decision make me a good ancestor?

Conscious living:

Finding a purpose outside of yourself has shown to be more beneficial for happiness than living purely for your own benefit.

Maybe you can find that one special activity that fulfils all these criteria:
- discover something you love doing
- think of something you're great at (or can become great at)
- seek out something you are rewarded for (rewards come in many different forms)
- find something the world needs

Which good-ancestor activities work for you?

- ☐ Campaign for an environmental cause
- ☐ Protect your local green space
- ☐ Hold a charity fundraiser
- ☐ Volunteer for a homeless shelter or refugee project
- ☐ Join your local conservation group
- ☐ Teach local children how to grow food
- ☐ Open your garden or allotment to visitors and give a tour
- ☐ Create and share environmental art, craft, music or literature
- ☐ Use computer or social media skills to promote a cause
- ☐ Join a befriending or mentoring service
- ☐ Use your skills to help others
- ☐ Check out 'Ikigai', a Japanese concept that means discovering and following your 'reason for being'

Your ideas:

☐

☐

☐

Explore your favourite
outdoor place

Note down words that you associate with it

Join those words to create a poem

Conscious living:

The words we use to describe the living world often lead us, consciously or unconsciously, to see ourselves as outside and superior to nature, rather than a part of it. When we use terms that disconnect us - such as 'ecosystem services' and 'pests and weeds' it becomes easier to destroy our world. If we use connected words - where humans see ourselves as part of the web of life - destruction appears unthinkable, just as we wouldn't consciously harm the people we love.

Many people are now changing their relationship with nature by changing the words that they use. We can learn from indigenous and native peoples, who often have a more connected language to describe their relationships with the rest of the living world, using terms like 'mother', 'father', 'cousin', 'brother', 'sister'. Indeed, many don't have words that separate humans from the rest of life at all.

Here are some ideas for different language we could choose:

- ☐ the rest of the living world
- ☐ other plants and animals
- ☐ the natural world
- ☐ the rest of life
- ☐ the more-than-human world
- ☐ the web of life
- ☐ our home
- ☐ our wild family
- ☐ all life
- ☐ cohabit
- ☐ places of natural wonder
- ☐ living planet
- ☐ our wild cousins
- ☐ all of nature, us included

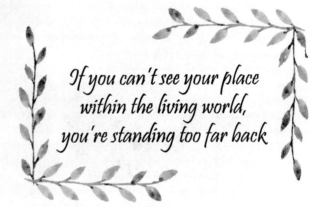

If you can't see your place within the living world, you're standing too far back

Be part of the natural world

We all have a fundamental need to belong, both amongst humans, but also within the rest of the living world. Shifting our thinking to that of connectedness increases our wellbeing and benefits the humans and other living beings that surround us. It's a positive spiral which satisfies a deep yearning, also known as 'biophilia'. This natural principle encourages us to nurture this connection by spending more time within the natural world and making an effort to see our wild cousins as part of our evolutionary family.

Complete the wreath in your own style to represent your unique place in the world.

Get to know a tree
through the seasons

Find a tree near you and visit it each month of the year. Record it in a sketch or photograph. Notice how your tree changes during the seasons. Record how your own mood, energy levels and body rhythms are changing with the seasons also. What wisdom does your tree have to share with you?

January

February

April

May

June

July

August

September

October

November

December

Natural rhythms...

Are you a night owl or a lark in your natural sleep patterns?

What is your body telling you?

How does your daily life reflect your natural rhythms?

How could you make them more in tune?

Tune in to natural cycles

We evolved while living outside and our bodily systems still operate according to the revolving timescales of our planet. If we observe our natural rhythms, such as the times we are tired, or when our mood changes, we can start to bring ourselves back into balance. Small changes can make a difference, such as experiencing early morning sunshine to help regulate your sleep patterns, or noticing when you are hungry or have had enough to eat.

Where does your food come from?

All our food originates as plants...
...helped by bees and other insects,
animals (including humans), plants and fungi

Conscious living:

Food growing, processing and transportation are huge contributors to climate change and biodiversity loss. By making simple change to our diet we, as individuals, can significantly lower our carbon footprint and help the plants and animals that share our world.

which of these are right for you and your circumstances?

- ☐ Aim for zero waste of any food you buy or grow
- ☐ Eat less (or no) meat or animal products
- ☐ Choose 100% grass fed local meat
- ☐ Eat chemical-free or organic food
- ☐ Give processed food and fast-food the boot
- ☐ Cook quick and easy meals from scratch with fresh ingredients
- ☐ Buy local and seasonal fruit and vegetables
- ☐ Avoid imported food, and especially food that has arrived by air
- ☐ Grow some of your own fruit and vegetables
- ☐ Create a herb garden or plant herbs in pots
- ☐ Preserve the harvest
- ☐ Creatively use leftovers
- ☐ Don't rely on 'sell-by' dates - use your own judgement
- ☐ Compost uncooked food
- ☐ Make a wormery for cooked food waste

Your ideas:

- ☐
- ☐
- ☐

Check out permaculture...

Permaculture is a design approach based on observations of how nature is successful. At its heart permaculture has three ethics and a set of principles inspired by natural systems.

This makes it a unique toolkit that is used to design regenerative systems at all scales - from home and garden to community, farms and bioregions around the world.

Through permaculture, people are treading lightly on our planet, in harmony with nature. By taking care of people and fellow creatures, we can ensure that we can sustain human activities for many generations to come.

Grow some food from seed

If you want the satisfaction of growing a whole meal here are some simple ideas:

Spring - stir-fry baby vegetables, stewed rhubarb
Summer - beetroot, pea and mixed leaf salad, fresh strawberries
Autumn - pumpkin soup, stewed damsons
Winter - leek and potato stew, baked apples

The three permaculture ethics:

One way to explore your relationship with the earth is to answer these questions.

Earth Care

How does the earth care for me?

How do I care for the earth?

People Care

How do other people care for me?

How do I care for other people?

Conscious living:

Abundance-thinking encourages us to look at the world in terms of bountifulness and plenty, realising when we have enough for our needs. This mindset is modelled on the abundance of the living world. The alternative is a scarcity mindset, where nothing is ever enough and we concentrate on what we don't have and on the failures we perceive within ourselves. This is often the mindset of the modern consumer society. The easiest way to cultivate an outlook of abundance is through gratitude - for yourself, the people around you and for the world. Additionally, the more we appreciate nature's abundance, the more we start to see what is truly important.

Fair Shares

How do others share with me?

How do I share with others?

Share the abundance

Apple trees, bursting with fruit, spread their seeds with the help of animals. The ripe fruit falls to the ground providing food for a multitude of organisms, large and small. In the natural world, the more living beings share, the richer the ecosystem becomes, creating spirals of abundance. This natural principle prompts us to share whatever surpluses we have too.

Make a nature mandala

Collect items from nature – leaves, twigs, flowers and other small bits and pieces.
Arrange them in a circular pattern, starting in the centre. Take your time.
Use the opportunity to clear your mind and concentrate solely on creating the pattern.
Recreate your mandala by doodling it here. Part of the joy of mandalas is knowing that
they will return to the earth after you've left.

My favourite nature books

Develop resilience

Trees teach us about resilience in many different ways.

Head outside and find ways that trees and other living beings demonstrate resilience.
Note or draw them on these pages.
Think about your own life – what might you learn from each example that you find?
(example: a tree actively heals the place where a branch has been cut, and we can make efforts to heal our bodies and our minds after trauma too).

Bend with the wind

There will always be things in our lives that we can't control. Even mighty oaks experience storms that shake their foundations. Visualising problems flowing through us, like wind through leaves and branches, can help to lessen anxiety in stressful situations and give us the strength to cope and thrive.

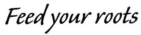

Feed your roots

Having strong 'roots' gives us inner strength and reserves for when times are tough. Roots can mean different things to different people. They might signify connection to a place, family or friends, or drawing strength from culture, spirituality and our own sense of purpose. Try to develop strong enough roots to allow you to care for yourself, but also to care for other people and to play your part in caring for all living beings.

The wood-wide web

Healthy soils contain miles of mycorrhizal fungi. This amazing web allows trees and other organisms to share resources, support each other and to communicate. Use these pages to doodle trees and their roots, then add the strands of fungi connecting the trees together.

"May my life be like a great
hospitable tree, and may
weary wanderers find
in me a rest."
~ John Henry Jowett

Cultivate co-operative relationships

We see mutually-beneficial relationships everywhere in nature, for example when we observe how bees pollinate flowers and receive nectar in return. In our own lives we can seek out friendships, collaborations and business opportunities. This involves building trust, learning effective communication skills and opening ourselves up to an element of risk and vulnerability.

Find examples of plants, animals, insects, fungi and other organisms co-operating with each other. Note ways that you can learn from each example for your own life.

Three things I appreciate

At the end of each day note three things you are grateful for:

1. Something about yourself
2. Something about another person
3. Something you appreciate about the living world and your part in it.

Saturday

Sunday

Monday

Tuesday

Wednesday

Thursday

Friday

100% in-nature challenge

Aim to engage with the rest of the living world 100% of the time.

Here are some ideas:

- ☐ Take a stroll during your lunch break
- ☐ Plant a pot or a window box with flowers or herbs
- ☐ Ask your boss to turn a disused space into a garden
- ☐ Share an allotment or join a community garden
- ☐ Cover your walls with paintings and photos of nature
- ☐ Wear flowery shirts and other clothing
- ☐ Place a pot plant in your office and bedroom
- ☐ Do some guerilla planting (planting secretly in disused urban spaces)
- ☐ Take a scenic walk to the shops
- ☐ Plant a small woodland garden in your back yard or in your local community
- ☐ Move your desk so you can see through a window whilst you're working
- ☐ Turn off your phone and your music when you are outside

Your ideas:

- ☐
- ☐
- ☐
- ☐
- ☐
- ☐
- ☐

"We do not inherit the Earth
from our ancestors,
we borrow it from our children"

More trees please!

Conscious living:

There are many ways you can contribute to the reforestation of our world.
Here are some ideas:

☐ Plant a tree in the ground or in a pot (if you only have a small area, planting the right variety will actually make your space look larger)
☐ Join your local community tree-planting scheme
☐ Ask the owner of your local green space if you can plant some trees or create a community orchard
☐ Sponsor trees (someone else will plant trees for you)
☐ Give trees as gifts and to mark significant events
☐ Use the Ecosia search engine (they plant trees for each internet search you do)
☐ Offset your carbon emissions with one of the offsetting schemes (but don't use this as an excuse for more carbon-heavy activities)
☐ Buy a piece of woodland or even part of the Amazon (thinking big here...)
☐ Look after any trees you already have, by giving them a mulch of compost or bark
☐ Join a conservation group to maintain your local woodlands and maximise their potential for biodiversity
☐ Buy used furniture and other products (so that you are not chopping down trees for your own consumption)
☐ If you buy new, always choose FSC(Forest Stewardship Council), or other trusted sources of certified wood.
☐ Respect and learn from indigenous and ancient knowledge
☐ Repurpose or upcycle your furniture and other wooden items
☐ Send unwanted furniture to a charity, thrift or second-hand shop
☐ Check out your local wood recycling scheme
☐ Switch to e-cards and re-usable gift wrapping
☐ Buy unpackaged food and other items
☐ But - consider when wood or paper might be better than the alternative (for example if it replaces plastic)
☐ Remember that tree-planting is great, but it's even more important to preserve our existing old trees and ancient woodlands
☐ Join campaigns to protect forests
☐ and finally, make the world better by living a simpler and happier life!

What are your next steps?

We hope that you have enjoyed the activities in this book and will continue to connect with nature and repeat the exercises at various times throughout the seasons. Please let us know which you particularly love and find useful.
Happy creating! from Sarah and Eva

Think like a Tree:
the natural principles guide to life
by Sarah Spencer

"Natural principles as a manual for the modern world"

Nature holds the secret to your happiness, health and wellbeing.
Now at last, you can unlock it.

We associate trees and woodlands with harmony, health and vitality. And yet, so often, we struggle to experience these qualities in our everyday lives.

What if we could harness the wisdom of the forest for ourselves?

Think like a Tree, the first guide of its kind, reveals the underlying principles of nature's secrets of success one by one, and demonstrates ways you can apply them to your own life, in this practical personal development guide.

These natural principles evolved over billions of years—they're the rules and patterns that all living things have in common for:

- finding purpose
- growth and success
- solving problems
- building resilience
- creating ideal conditions to thrive
- developing positive relationships
- leaving a lasting legacy

Drawing on woodland examples from around the globe, Think like a Tree shares the amazing abilities of trees, their evolutionary success stories and their abilities to heal.

This book guides you to discover your own personal route to happiness, health, success and fulfilment—whatever your circumstances.

The natural principles, harnessed from observations in nature, can be used for:

- wellbeing
- physical health
- psychological health and happiness
- overcoming a life-challenge
- motivation
- coping with stress
- anxiety and depression
- transforming your life
- relationship problems
- work-life balance
- planning for the future
- and more!

Throughout the book author Sarah Spencer shares her inspirational real-life story of health recovery - how she used the natural principles to overcome significant illness, find her purpose and achieve happiness. She now spends her time inspiring others to use trees and nature to design the life they want to lead via books, workshops and online courses.

Available in paperback and ebook from Amazon, bookstores and ebook retailers.

Signed copies direct from the author at www.thinklikeatree.co.uk

Inspired by Acorns

Activity book for kids

by Sarah Spencer and Eva Spencer

Packed with activities, inspiring quotes and eco ideas, with plenty of space for writing, drawing, making, thinking and learning.

For ages 4 to 12.

Use as a stand-alone book, or parents and children can complete activity books together.

Parents can enjoy *Inspired by Trees* and children can enjoy *Inspired by Acorns,* with parallel activities and illustrations for parent and child on each page, benefitting parents' and childrens' mental and physical health and wellbeing simultaneously.

Must-have books for every outdoor trip.

Think like a Tree courses and workshops

❐   Think like a Tree programme:

This unique course puts the natural principles into action in a practical step-by-step way using a design cycle that can be used for everyone's circumstances. Online or in beautiful woodland locations.

❐   Think like a Tree workshops on a range of themes (online and in person)
❐   Children and family workshops
❐   Corporate activities
❐   Workshops at festivals and events

Turn your passion for nature into a career

Train as a Think like a Tree facilitator and offer the Think like a Tree programme, courses and workshops in your own venue. Join an enthusiastic group of facilitators offering courses in many locations and for many different ages and audiences. Integrate into your existing specialism or interests.

www.thinklikeatree.co.uk

Join the email list via the website to receive details of forthcoming books, courses, workshops, free giveaways and other tree-related stuff...

Facebook @thinklikeatree   Instagram @thinklikeatree   Twitter @thinklikeatree5
Email: sarah@thinklikeatree.co.uk

About

Sarah and Eva are mother and daughter from South Derbyshire in the centre of the UK. Sarah, her husband Roger, their three children, and Sarah's parents, bought a smallholding in 2003 and have since developed and nurtured it using permaculture, organic and other sustainable principles.

Over the years they have created woodlands, orchards, vegetable plots and gardens for cut flowers. They keep chickens, and bees using natural beekeeping methods. Their land is in the National Forest, a forest they have seen grow from saplings to large trees, and a project they have been proud to be part of. Sarah and Eva have both been actively involved in creating a community woodland social-enterprise called Whistlewood Common and Sarah trained as a forest school leader and holds a Diploma in Applied Permaculture Design.

Eva grew up surrounded by trees, helping out on the land during evenings and weekends, and camping with friends in the fields to celebrate birthdays and other special occasions. She has since graduated from university and moved to London for her work with charities. In the city she seeks out local parks and enjoys painting in her spare time.

Sarah shares the wisdom of nature through Think like a Tree courses and workshops. Mother and daughter love attending festivals where they can share their passion for nature and promote the importance of taking urgent action on climate change and other environmental issues.

If you've enjoyed this book we've a favour to ask...

Connecting people with nature is our passion and we believe in creating collaborations and connections (just like the mycorrhizal networks that connect trees).

If that's something that you are passionate about too, we'd love your help:

- ❑ Please leave an impartial review on Amazon and/or Goodreads.
- ❑ Tell your friends and famiy about the books. They make great gifts too!
- ❑ Share, like and comment on Think like a Tree's posts on social media.
- ❑ Share photos of your workbook on your own social media pages, tagging Think like a Tree.
- ❑ If you have a green therapy/outdoor/green/eco business please get in touch for bulk purchase/ commission rates for our books.
- ❑ Invite us to contribute to your blog, podcast, website, magazine etc.
- ❑ Invite us to run a workshop at your festival, event or workplace.

www.thinklikeatree.co.uk

Printed in Great Britain
by Amazon